For the Love of Animals

The story of Heather Moorse
and Sunnyridge Animal Rescue

**Recorded, transcribed and written
by Jenny Peet**

Previous books by Jenny Peet

Village Voices - Charlton Horethorne
Town Tales - Wincanton

First published in 2007 by Tomorrow's History
Pippin Cottage
North Road
Charlton Horethorne
Sherborne
Dorset
DT9 4NS
peet.pippin@virgin.net

ISBN 0-9552430-2-5
978-0-9552430-2-8

Further copies of this book can be obtained from
Heather Moorse
Greenfields
Pound Lane
Gillingham
Dorset
SP8 4NP

Printed by Remous Ltd., Milborne Port, Sherborne Dorset DT9 5EP

Acknowledgements

My thanks are due to Maggie Baker for the front and back cover photographs; to Ken Parradine for his wonderful cartoons; to Crossroads Pet Supplies for their generosity over the years; to the Western Gazette Newspaper for helping to publicise the work of Sunnyridge Animal Rescue; to Dr Mark Newton-Clarke of Swan House Animal Hospital; to the very many volunteers who worked tirelessly for Sunnyridge and to Jenny Peet for listening patiently to my memories for many hours and for making my dream of writing a book come true.

"I dedicate this book to Peter for his love and for giving me the confidence to record my memories. Also to my children, for living with the constant upheaval caused by caring for so many animals and birds, and to my grandchildren that they may learn and gain compassion from these true stories."

Swan House Animal Hospital
Lower Acreman Street
SHERBORNE
Dorset DT9 3EX

Tel: 01935 816228
Fax: 01935 815802
Email: markn-c.vet@zen.co.uk

Date: 19/07/07

Heather Moorse dedicated her life to the welfare of animals, mostly rescued from people no longer willing or able to look after their own pets. Countless rabbits, guinea pigs, chinchillas and other small, defenceless creatures were given the chance of life at Heather's home in the tiny hamlet of Stowell. Housing, feeding and caring for literally hundreds of small animals became Heather's way of life, all of it supported only by her own fundraising efforts. Heather's reputation for compassion and dedication spread over much of South Somerset and Dorset and will almost certainly never be matched, much to the disadvantage of all unwanted animals in this area. It was a privilege to serve as Heather's veterinary surgeon for eight years and I wish her a very happy and much-deserved retirement.

MARK NEWTON-CLARKE
MA VetMB PhD MRCVS

From the Somerset East Branch of the RSPCA

Where do you start with Heather?

I have had the pleasure of knowing her for over 30 years. Our first meeting was when she asked to adopt the most beautiful longhaired cream kitten. I remember walking into her sitting room to be faced with the whole family sitting in a semi-circle waiting for this delight. They were made to sit quietly while the kitten was allowed to meet them. No messing, no misbehaviour - they were all devoted animal lovers and Heather was in control.

Over the years we have remained firm friends and if I had a sister I would wish it to be Heather. Even when years went by with little contact I was always made welcome whenever I appeared and made to feel almost like family. There were always people coming and going, buying eggs or rare breeds of chickens from Peter, asking for advice or bringing in a sick or injured wild bird or small mammal for Heather to care for. Both Heather and Peter had a wealth of knowledge that compared favourably with the many books written on the rehabilitation of wild animals.

Heather never had a lot of money but I always marvelled at how far she could make it go, far better than I could ever manage. No one ever went without tea or cake and no animal was every hungry. From time to time the RSPCA Somerset East Branch paid for a little food for the animals or the occasional veterinary fee, it was always accepted reluctantly but if an animal needed the care, it was taken.

Every living thing had the same care and attention - particularly Peter and the children. The garden became overrun with various pens, runs, cages and aviaries. I know the hours involved took over Heather's working day mentally and physically. Occasionally Heather and I would give ourselves a treat and escape for the day on a gardening trip, Heather's second love. Her garden was always a riot of colour, her greenhouses full of growing seedlings or cuttings that flourished under her green fingers.

None of us ever thought that she would leave Stowell, but it has given her a new lease of life with less work to do and time to remember her stories that entertained us when time permitted. Enjoy these stories - there are not many people like her with love and time for everything and everyone. She deserves a rest, well apart from recalling her memories for us all to enjoy.

After all her years of dedication I was proud to put her name forward to receive the RSPCA Queen Victoria bronze medal in 2006 in honour of her work. I can think of no one who was better qualified to receive it.

Maggie Baker
Honorary Branch Treasurer and Welfare Officer for Somerset East Branch of the RSPCA and Council member of the National Society of the RSPCA.

This is to certify
that the

Queen Victoria Bronze Medal

of the

ROYAL SOCIETY
FOR THE PREVENTION OF
CRUELTY TO ANIMALS

has been awarded to

Mrs H Moorse

for her long and meritorious
service in the cause of animal welfare

Date: 5th April 2006   Chairman, RSPCA Council

A lonely childhood

I was born in 1938 near Corton Denham in South Somerset where my mother had been in service at the big house there. Within six weeks my mother and I had moved down to Lustleigh in South Devon to join my father who worked on the railways before starting his own little business as a cobbler. He was a hard, cruel man who came from Sunderland, where he had been a coal miner, and during the Depression had moved down to Devon to find work

I can remember the cottage in Devon so well. It was a thatched cottage, very tiny, and it flooded every winter because it was near a stream. As a small child one of my jobs was to help to drag sandbags to the front of the house in an attempt to keep out the water. But they didn't do much good, they didn't stop the flow of water into the hall and kitchen, and for much of the time the cottage felt cold and damp.

I was an only child and had no other children near by to play with. My friends were the animals and birds and they took the place of brothers and sisters. They were, and still are, my whole life, along with my husband and children whom I adore.

I had complete freedom to roam. My parents liked whippets and I had a whippet of my own when I was two years old and he would accompany me out into the woods, uncovering all kinds of fascinating creatures as he snuffled in the undergrowth. I knew exactly where the rabbits lived, where the thrushes built their nests, the route the foxes took on their nightly trek across our garden and often returned to the kitchen with a bunch of wild flowers clutched tightly in my hand.

We lived in Lustleigh until I was about eight years old and I attended the village school. I was very unhappy there because the teachers constantly bullied me; I was the underdog. I was lonely and very shy, and the other children blamed me for what went wrong, probably because I didn't know how to stick up for myself.

My father was an absolute brute and my mother was very frightened of him. He never hit us but his temper and attitude terrified me. If there was a row my parents wouldn't talk to each other for weeks on end and there was I, a tiny child, acting as the go-between. I could feel the atmosphere, you could cut it with a knife, and I dreaded what he might do to my mother or me. I was absolutely petrified.

© *Ken Parradine*

Plop, plop, plop

It was late one night, round about eleven o'clock, when we heard a large vehicle being reversed into the farmyard. 'Have you ordered something I don't know about?' I asked Peter, my husband. 'No,' said Peter scratching his head, 'We'd better take a look at what's happening out there.' We stuffed our feet into our welly boots grabbed our torches and strode out into the pitch-black night. There were, and still are, no street lights in many of the villages and hamlets in this unspoilt area of South Somerset and without a good bright torch getting around can be quite tricky.

I threw open the back door and there in the yard stood a cattle dealer's large truck. 'What the hell are you bringing us at this hour?' I shouted as I stamped across the muddy yard to put on the outside lights. 'It's a bit late to be delivering cattle, isn't it?' 'He's a nice little beast for you to rear,' answered George as the rain dripped off his flat cap, 'I have a load of Jerseys to collect at six in the morning so you have to have him tonight.'

He dropped down the van tailgate and out into the farmyard shot this ten-month-old bull calf which had just come off its mother. He was as wild as could be, kicking, snorting, tossing his head and wouldn't let us go anywhere near him. We occasionally took in single animals like this. Not many people could be bothered to do it. Rearing one animal for market is a lot of hard work - but it did enable us to earn much needed cash.

'Fetch the ropes,' instructed Peter. Time and again we tried to lassoo him but he was too quick for us. He'd had the freedom of the fields far too long and was not as docile as most calves. You couldn't blame him really because he'd been happily feeding from his mother for all those months and then suddenly had been dragged away from her, shut up in a smelly and noisy truck and then turned out into an alien environment. Poor creature.

Round and round the yard he clattered, steaming with sweat, eyes bulging. Peter threw open the door to the shed, the bull calf galloped in and the door was slammed shut. Peter took off his cap, rubbed his head dry, and said, 'That's enough exercise for one night. By morning he'll be fine - ready for a good feed.'

The following morning we opened the shed door, the calf shot out like a bullet from a gun, and jumped clean over a five bar gate. We ran after him but he was off cantering down the lane at such a speed we hadn't a cat in hell's chance of catching him. We jumped into the car and drove frantically up and down the lanes searching for the bull calf but he'd disappeared. 'What the hell do we do now?' I asked Peter. 'We'd better let the police know first and then we'll just have to phone all the farms round about.' But nobody had seen him.

Three days later we had a phone call from a farmer's wife up the hill,' Heather, I think we have your yearling in with our cows. Can you come and catch him?' 'You won't believe this,' I said, looking at myself in the mirror, 'I've just got myself dressed up for the first time in weeks. I'm meeting a friend in Sheborne for lunch but I'll just have enough time to come up and collect him before I go.'

Peter and I climbed into the old post office van that Peter had bought at a sale. 'This'll only take a few minutes,' said Peter, 'Then you'll be off with plenty of time to spare.' I felt far too smart to be chasing cattle; I was dressed for the shops in a beautiful new pale pink jumper and black trousers.

It took us two whole hours to catch the blessed thing and eventually, with a rope around its neck we pulled it back to the van. 'You sit in the back of the van, Peter, and I'll drive. Hold the bugger tight and what ever you do don't let it turn round with its bottom near me.' The calf had been grazing in a field of fresh young grass and had eaten well. When you put young cows and calves out on pasture as lush as that they get what we call the scours, which is very bad diarrhoea.

I was driving past the village church when there was a hell of a rumpus in the back of the van. The vehicle rocked so much I was in danger of crashing as Peter, shouting at the top of his voice, tried to control the struggling calf. The next minute I felt plop, plop, plop right on the top of my head. Green scours, slimy, stinking and steaming, cascaded over my head, running down behind my ears, down my neck, in between my shoulder blades right down to my bottom. The stench was unbelievable.

I drove home as fast as I could, slammed on the brakes so hard that you could see the skid marks on the road for months, and ran dripping towards the house shouting as I went, 'You can sort the bugger out now.' Grabbing a pair of scissors off the stack of feed bags I hacked off every piece of clothing I was wearing and ran naked across the farmyard for a long hot bath. I never thought I'd smell sweet again and I didn't get to Sherborne that day.

Toffee treats

Needing extra land we rented some pastureland, out towards Charlton Horethorne, on which we grazed three beautiful Jersey cows. Twice each day we collected them to bring them back for milking - their names were Daisy, Marigold and Queenie. Although Jerseys look gentle, obedient creatures they can become very stubborn when it's time to round them up. The only way I could get them to do exactly as I wanted was to stuff my pockets with toffees and at the first sign of any trouble out the sweets would come to be fed to them. They loved toffees and at the first sniff of one cradled in the palm of my hand the cows would become as obedient as well trained pussycats. As long as I had a bag of them in my pocket they would follow me to the end of the world.

One day the decision was made to send them on to market, never an easy decision, but it's one that has to be faced. The following day I carefully washed and cleaned the cows, milked them and made sure they were ready for collection.

The cattle drover duly arrived and reversed his truck up the farmyard, dropped the tailgate, climbed inside and out he jumped brandishing in his hands one of those cruel electric cattle prods, the kind that delivers a sharp stinging pain. With hands on hips he stood glowering at me, cracking the prod irritably against his leg. 'Come on,' he said, 'Where's these animals? I can't wait around all day. I've got another three farms to visit.' Then he spotted the Jerseys waiting patiently in the corner of the yard. Moving towards them, the instrument of torture primed to do its job he growled, 'I'll soon get 'em up,' and determinedly he marched towards them.

The cows backed away trembling, starting to panic with fear. I wasn't having my cows treated like this so running between him and the cows I blocked his path, stopping his advancement. 'No, you won't soon get them up,' I shouted, 'You won't use that prodder on my cows.' Chin sticking out, squaring his shoulders ready to fight, he growled back, 'I'll do what I like, missus. I've come to collect these cows and I'll do it anyway I like.' This small, mean looking man was a cruel, bad tempered bully. But many times I'd stuck up to bullies for my animals, and I was to do so again. I bellowed even louder, 'You don't do what you like here, mister. If you use that cattle prong on my Jerseys I will stick it up your arse. Get off, and never, ever, come back to this farm.'

He was so shocked he was speechless. He scurried back into his cab as quickly as his little legs could carry him, scrambled aboard and drove out of the farmyard as if the hounds of hell were snapping at his heels. The cows, which had skittered into a corner, had to be calmed and soothed until another carrier could be found. Calmed with a generous supply of toffees this time they boarded the truck happy and content.

© Ken Parradine

Beady little eyes

There we were, back where I was born, in Stafford's Green sharing a house with my grandparents. I found out by accident that my father had TB and nobody thought it was important to tell me he was ill. As he couldn't work for some time we were very dependent upon the generosity of my mother's parents.

My grandmother was a huge lady, about twenty stones in weight, and my grandfather was tiny. There were other grandchildren in the family and, when they came to visit, grandma would bring out tins of sweets and boxes of chocolates. With a big smile on her face she would offer my cousins a delicious choice. But I was never offered one, I had to stand by and suffer in silence as my cousins sucked and chomped away at their little treats. Grandma would put her hands on her capacious hips, look straight into my eyes, and say, 'You're not having any.' My mother stood there silently, never questioning, never sticking up for me, just accepting her mother's decision. We were living with my grandparents and they were in charge.

My grandfather was a rabbit catcher and he had bought the rights to hunt rabbits on Cadbury Castle land and all the land around several farms in the area. He set off each day with his ferrets and at the end of the day would return home with a long branch full of strung up dead rabbits. At the back of the house there were branches and branches of dead rabbits, all waiting to be sold, it was horrendous. Every day I was faced with seeing my rabbit friends suspended there, eyes bulging, blood dripping, waiting to be collected by local butchers.

The toilet at the cottage was just a bucket in a stone outhouse which was situated at the end of a long and slippery path at the bottom of the garden. Grandad kept his ferrets in cages in the outhouse, he had about twenty of them, and they sat there watching me use the bucket with their little beady eyes glowing brightly in the torchlight. I was terrified and put off 'paying a call' as long as I could. In the winter I was terrified as my torchlight illuminated these vicious little beasts which looked as if they were longing to grab me by the neck and bite me to death, as they did the rabbits.

One day, as I was sitting on the bucket with my knickers round my ankles, I heard a sound and spied an escaped ferret in the corner of the outhouse. I was frozen with fear and didn't know what to do. The slinky brilliant eyed creature spied me sitting there, launched itself at me, and bit deeply into my hand. With the ferret firmly clinging onto to my hand I screeched, howled, and shouted and tried to bash it against the wall to dislodge it but nobody could hear me. I leaped off the bucket and with my knickers round my ankles I hobbled all the way down the garden with the ferret still attached to me. Howling at the top of my voice I stumbled into the kitchen but nobody could see why I was making such a fuss. Unceremoniously grandad squeezed the ferret's mouth open to release it from my hand and stroking it lovingly and coo-ing to it as if it had suffered some great injury, he carried it back to its cage.

Ferrets are the only animals I don't like and it takes me all my time nowadays to even touch one.

I DID'NT GO TO THE LOO, JUST TO GET YOU !

Trouble with a bit of skirt

Going to market to sell animals is not always a pleasant experience and there are times when it can be very distressing. Selling on stock lovingly reared was not always easy because there was often an element of cruelty at the market which I could not abide.

One day at Sturminster Newton market Peter went off to view the cattle leaving me to watch the proceedings. As I was leaning on the rails watching the auction I heard more shouting and swearing than usual and looking up I spotted a drover driving some animals towards the auction ring. He was a mean faced evil looking little man who appeared to be enjoying beating the cattle as hard as he could with his big stout stick. His brown overalls and black wellington boots were plastered with mud and animal dung. Hearing each crack land on the backs of the defenceless cows my temper started to rise. I felt like Vesuvius ready to blow.

The drover worked himself into a frenzy beating and beating one of the animals which wouldn't move into the ring. It was a badly neglected creature, under fed and covered in its own excrement, bellowing in pain as it tried to escape the blows raining down on it. I couldn't stand just there doing nothing - I'd seen enough.

I flew through the gate of the cattle ring and marched right up to the drover but before I could say anything he shrieked at me, 'What the hell do you want? Get out of the way, I've another load of cows to get in here after this lot have been sold. Go on, move.' 'You shouldn't be hitting the cows like that,' I shouted as loudly as I could, 'It's so cruel and unnecessary.' 'What's it to do with you, Missus?' he roared at me as he turned and continued to lay into the animal with his stick. 'I have feelings for animals and I know the pain they suffer when you treat them like that' I argued. 'How would you like me to take that stick and beat you as hard as you are beating that cow?' 'Just you try,' he smirked. The challenge was too much to resist and grasping the stick firmly I tried to wrestle it from his grip.

The crowd was delighted by this unexpected entertainment and the numbers of spectators started to multiply. To see a drover being confronted by a woman in such an unexpected way caused great merriment. Then the jeering started and the atmosphere turned very unpleasant. 'Having a spot of trouble with a bit of skirt,' one old farmer shouted. 'Go on, love, give him one,' joined in somebody else. 'Women shouldn't be allowed in here,' bellowed a voice from the back of the crowd. Now the crowd hadn't thought about that before and with general assent they began shouting for me to be thrown out of the cattle ring.

Struggling to get control of the stick I cried out loudly, 'I don't believe animals should be beaten till they're on their knees. I'm going to show you what it feels like.' Everyone burst out laughing. Suddenly the drover's muddy hands let slip of the stick and grasping it firmly I raised it in the air.

I was just about to hit him as hard as I could across the shoulders when over the loud speakers a voice was heard shouting, 'Peter Moorse, come and get your bloody wife and don't bring her to this market again.'

© *Ken Parradine*

cows because Peter had to go and milk somebody else's cows afterwards to make a bit of extra money. The plan was to get the ten new cows milked before going off to his 'client'. These new cows had never, ever been tied up in a cow stall in their lives, let alone had a chain fastened around their necks. They had been milked in a milking bale out in the fields. Usually when you put a chain round a cow's neck it just stands there patiently because it knows it is going to be fed whilst being milked.

Seven of the cows were not too bad; we got them in and tied them up successfully and put the chains around their necks to hold them in place. Cows are ungainly animals so Peter had to push them in position from behind and it was my job to put on the chains. The last three animals were terrible. They wouldn't shift.

Peter pushed one of them as hard as he could, he shoved and shouted at me in frustration but I just couldn't get the chain round the animal's neck. In exasperation he gave an almighty push and shouted, 'For God's sake, woman, get the bloody cow tied up.' The chain pulled tight round my fingers, Peter was pushing with all his might, the cow was pulling in the opposite direction, and there was a loud snap. My wrist dangled on the end of my arm at a crazy angle with a bone sticking right out of the skin in a completely different direction to which bones usually lay. I screamed, 'Peter, I think my wrist's broken.' 'It doesn't matter about your blasted wrist, just get them tied up,' He bellowed. He hadn't seen it then because he was more interested in getting the cows tied up; when he did he was very sorry. I ended up with my wrist in a plaster cast for eight very long and trying weeks.

© Ken Parradine

Broken tails

Before we married, although I was very happy working for Major Yockney, I was asked to manage a farm ten miles away at Buckhorn Weston. This farmer had sixty pedigree Friesian cows, sixty followers (young calves) and two bulls. I jumped at the offer and went to live over at the farm; my parents came with me, and almost every penny I earned had to be handed over to them.

We milked in cow stalls then; the milk going into ten gallon churns. On my first morning the cows walked into the cow-stall to be milked as placid as usual. But when I switched on the milking machine each and every one of them started to shake, their eyes bulged with fear. I'd never seen anything like this before. I was horrified. 'Have they got some strange disease?' I wondered.

Starting at the head of the first cow I methodically checked every part of her body, coming finally to her tail. There lay the answer. The tail had three breaks in it. I went on to examine the next cow - that had seven breaks in its tail. Along the line I progressed, being as gentle as I could with each shaking animal. Each cow had a suffered a broken tail, most of them had three breaks, but some had up to eight.

Standing there I pondered this strange problem and then the penny dropped; this was how the dairyman had controlled his cows during milking. If they didn't co-operate he would grab them by the tail and break them to force them into submission.

Over the next few weeks I milked my cows with infinite tenderness, talking to them all the time and reassuring them. Within two months I had them all quiet. I was very happy and loved my work. The local farmers thought I was very funny, treating my cows so gently, but they were laughing on the other side of their faces because within six months the milk yield from my happy cows was up by half!

THIS IS 'KNOT' THE WAY
MY TAIL SHOULD BE!

© Ken Parradine

Tasty Toes

Pinky and Perky were two runts; piglets that were weak, undernourished and not expected to survive. I had a way with pigs and more often than not managed to raise them to good health. Pinky and Perky were kept nice and snug by the side of the Rayburn cooker in the kitchen and I fed them cow's milk through a teat on a baby's bottle. They had the most beautiful pink shiny coats and it was a joy to stoke their warm hairy little bodies. I groomed them and dusted them down with baby powder each day and they smelled delicious. Every time they heard my voice, even if they were fast asleep, their ears would prick up and they'd start squealing at the top of their voices to be picked up.

Wherever I went in the house they followed me; even the stairs presented no problem to them and they scrambled up after me with boundless enthusiasm. I got used to their scampering up and down the house like a couple of young puppies.

One evening I left Peter sound asleep in front of the fire, his stockinged feet stretched out towards the heat, and went into the bedroom to hang up some newly ironed clothes. I hadn't been there for long when I heard the most tremendous screaming and shouting coming from the sitting room. Hurrying in I saw Peter hopping up and down the room desperately trying to shake Perky off his foot. Perky had seen Peter's pink toe sticking through a hole in his sock and had thought it was a teat, and his teeth were clamped on nice and tight. The noise was unbelievable, Peter shrieking, the pigs squealing and I in fits of laughter. 'Don't you ever dare have any more pigs in this house,' Peter instructed, 'That damned thing has bitten my toe.'

The following morning Peter woke up early as usual and went down to the kitchen. A short time later I followed and to my amazement there he was, standing on one of the kitchen chairs, drinking a cup of tea. 'I'm not standing down there with baby pigs lose,' he complained, 'They go for my toes!'

© Ken Parradine

Illness strikes

Being an only child I wanted to have a large family, my own family to care for and cherish. I soon had two very happy and healthy children, Susan and young Peter. When I was four months pregnant with Robert, my third child, I woke up one Saturday morning with what I thought was a dreadful migraine. 'I'll just lie here quietly,' I thought. 'I'll soon feel better.' After a while I decided to get out of bed and to my horror I found I couldn't stand. What on earth was the matter with me? I'd been poorly before but I'd never had anything like this.

Bringing a cup of tea to the bedside Peter took one look at me and said, 'You're staying in bed today, you look as though you have a really bad dose of flu. I'll look after you. The children can go round to my mother's; you need a really good rest.' I lay there trying not to panic but as the day wore on I felt worse and worse until I couldn't feel my feet, and then I couldn't feel my legs, I was losing the ability to move and I was terrified.

Doctor Goddard, our kind and rather eccentric GP, came about seven o'clock at night carrying a gun, which he put on the table - he'd been attacked a few nights previously and so carried a gun on his rounds. We understood each other implicitly; he had been a shy child like me, and had to fight to get to where he wanted to be. He took one look at me, shook his head, and said, 'Heather, if you'd been an animal I'd have used my gun and put you out of your misery.' I had to laugh, even though I was feeling desperately ill.

He opened his Gladstone bag, got out some sharp pins and proceeded to push them into my feet, then into my legs and then right up to my waist. I couldn't feel a thing. He looked me between the eyes and said, 'Heather, I think you might have polio.'

KILL OR CURE

© Ken Parradine

Inky

The little grey bird lay in my hand, all skin and bones. 'It'll never survive.' I thought. I started feeding it first on bread and milk, then on meal worms from the pet shop, and finally on tinned, watered down dog food, which is very good for baby birds. Experience taught me that the best way to feed baby birds is with a paintbrush, anything else can easily damage the beak.

Whenever I feed birds and animals I always talk to them. Sometimes it can be a bit exasperating, especially when they're slow to feed, so time and again I would say to the bird, 'Come on. Come on quick.' To start off with I kept him in a little box, and then in a cage as he grew bigger and his feathers started to come. 'It looks like a blackbird, but it's growing too big,' I thought. 'That's a flipping jackdaw,' said Peter. The bird's dark feathers shone with good health as he flitted up and down the garden. 'We'll call him Inky,' I said to the children and Inky became one of the most fascinating birds I've ever reared.

One afternoon we had visitors coming to visit so tidying up I popped Inky in his cage in one of the bedrooms out of the way. As I was walking down the passageway I heard someone say, 'Come on, come on quick,' and thinking it was the visitors who'd arrived early I rushed into the kitchen to greet them. The room was empty. I looked through the open window but no-one was there - I was the only person at home; it was very puzzling.

I walked back into the bedroom and there was Inky with his head on one side looking up at me. I looked back at him, 'No', I thought, 'It can't be. It can't have been Inky talking.' But it was. They always used to say that to get a jackdaw to talk you had to split its tongue. That is such a cruel thing to do. Inky's uncut tongue certainly didn't prevent him from talking and he became a wonderful mimic.

I can't abide seeing birds caged up so Inky was allowed to fly around the house. He was such a bright intelligent creature and would land on the sink draining board, shake his feathers and say, 'Come on, come on quick, Mum,' and he'd stay there squawking until I filled the sink for him to bathe in. Then he'd jump in, wash his feathers with great gusto, and jump out again shaking his feathers vigorously up and down the kitchen.

When he was young, as I walked around the farm, he'd sit companionably on my shoulder. Then he started to fly off on his own and come back with bits of kitchen foil or any sparkly piece he'd found. Jackdaws are terrible thieves and will pick up anything small that sparkles. I dreaded him coming back with anything valuable so we built him a big aviary, planted a grapevine to grow over it, and erected him a little house on the end.

Inky lived for fourteen years and his vocabulary increased as the years passed. When we had visitors he would greet them with, 'Good morning,' 'How are you today?' He was fascinating and could come out with the right words at the right time.

During the hunting season the Blackmore Vale Hunt met at the kennels in the next village, Charlton Horethorne. Quite a few of the hunting gentry in their red or black coats rode through our hamlet on their way to join the hunt. If I was working outside in the garden I'd call out, 'Good morning,' but usually they ignored me and clattered past without speaking. I knew most of these people well but the putting on of a smart black or red hunting jacket seemed to alter their whole personality.

Inky loved shouting out at people walking or riding nearby. One morning a very pompous, florid complexioned gentleman in his red hunting jacket came riding past with his nose stuck right up in the air. Peter and I were working away together and I called my usual greeting. The rider looked at us as if we were just bits of mud on the ground and didn't bother to reply. When he got to our driveway I heard Inky shout loud and clear, 'Good morning.' To my amazement the rider doffed his hat and replied in a very gentlemanly way, 'Good morning,' and rode on! I bet he'd have been surprised if he'd known he was talking to a jackdaw.

© Ken Parradine

Isolated

'I'm sorry, Heather,' said Dr Goddard, 'My suspicions were right. I'm sorry, but you have polio.' I was dumbstruck. 'What about the children? What about Peter? And what about the farm? How will we manage?' I asked. 'The children and farm will be no problem. Peter's family is going to step in to help and all you have to do is concentrate on getting better. The ambulance will be here to collect you shortly.' 'I suppose I'm going into Yeovil hospital - at least that won't be too far for visitors.' 'Oh, Heather,' said Dr Goddard, 'I'm sorry but the only hospital with an isolation unit is in Bristol.' Bristol was a 40 mile journey along mainly country roads.

The ambulance took me to the Ham Green Isolation Unit at Bristol Hospital where most of the polio patients were being treated in iron lungs. Being four months pregnant I was desperately worried about my unborn child. Most of the doctors seemed to want to ignore that; they were primarily concerned, understandably, with the disease. I asked an English doctor, 'What will happen to my baby? Do you think it will be all right?' He said, 'If it's born all right it will be immune to everything.' That was all I was told. I had the best attention from the black nurses and doctors; they were brilliant; they always had time to spend with me.

An isolation room is a very lonely place. There were no other patients to talk to, I couldn't move much, and the only thing I had plenty of was time. As I lay there I listened for the early morning call of the blackbird, and all the stories of my pets would walk before my eyes. I could remember each and every one of them. I couldn't see out of the window from where I was but I could recall all the birds, their songs, their nesting; each dog I had ever cared for, the rabbits gambolling in the fields, the cows, and the green, green fields, and most of all Peter and my children. I'm sure that it was these thoughts that helped me to get better.

Peter was working all the hours he could on the farm, was caring for our other two small children with the help of his mother, and it was a very long way for him to drive to visit me. Fortunately the disease was caught in time, I didn't need an iron lung, and very gradually I started to get the feeling back from the waist down. Then one day I made the decision to take my life into my own hands and when Peter came I discharged myself.

My baby got bigger and bigger; I got fatter and fatter. I was almost as wide as I was tall. My shoulders were so huge they would get stuck into the car door. Robert was born on 30 December, a perfect beautiful baby, and has been immune to everything, just as the doctor predicted.

© Ken Parradine

Turning over the pages of the local newspaper I spotted an advert for domestic staff in an old people's nursing home. 'I could do that,' I thought, 'I'm really well qualified by now.' Having to care for three generations in one household had taught me a great deal about patience and diplomacy. I phoned the Matron of the home, went for an interview, and soon found myself working for a wage - at long last.

I was a general dogsbody and to start off I enjoyed my work very much. It was good to get away from my own house, and my own 'old people,' to see fresh faces and to hear about other people's lives. But there's only so much cleaning, washing people, helping to feed them, taking them to the toilet, you can do and after a time I felt in need of a change. I was, after all, simply replicating what would be waiting for me at home when I hung up my work apron.

Then I spotted an advert for a cleaner for a lady in the village who had black retriever dogs. She kept twelve of them, and was very high up in showing at competitions like Crufts. It was my job to go up there, clean out the kennels, and scrub the kitchen and house floors.

Although the dogs had outdoor kennels to live in they mainly lived in the house and trying to keep the stone kitchen floor clean was a nightmare. It was unbelievable. I would be there on my hands and knees and, without thinking about me, the lady would let the retrievers out into the thick mud where they would play around and come running straight back on my damp newly cleaned kitchen floor. Within five minutes you wouldn't know I'd been busy.

The place was a nightmare. There were dishes of stinking dog food everywhere; sometimes meat, sometimes tripe, and then there were the water bowls cluttering up the floor all of which would be knocked around by the hungry animals spilling their contents. It was crazy but I loved it. It was a job and we were desperate for money.

But of course working for someone else meant that I had to be away from home and when I returned I always had to catch up on the jobs that I'd had to leave before going out to work. I pondered this. 'There must be some solution,' I thought.

Then one day I had a brilliant idea - we had a very large farmhouse with rooms to spare so I decided to take in lodgers. Each weekday I provided bed, breakfast and evening meal, for £3 per night, for fourteen Plessey employees who were working locally. It made a big difference to our family budget.

© Ken Parradine

**A poem from the very first lodger at Sunnyridge -
a very satisfied customer.**

'Twas a pleasure to meet you. Heather and Pete
I've had the most wonderful stay
My only regret, and that's life I expect
Is the fact that I'm leaving today!

Ken Parradine

50

Milking time for Peter

Sunnyridge bungalow - when we moved in

Major, Mimi and Martha

It had been a beautiful early summer day and, being late afternoon, it was time to round up the cows for milking. They were on pastureland a short distance from the farm and in the field next to the cows I kept my two female donkeys, Mimi who was three weeks short of foaling, and Martha who would follow on with her foal a couple of months later. They shared the pasture with my horse and a jack donkey I was looking after for a friend.

Whenever I collected the cows I always checked on the donkeys and on this particular day they were fine, happily grazing away as usual. I gave them each a handful of nuts, patted their rumps, rounded up the cows and walked them to the milking parlour. As I milked the cows something kept niggling at the back of my mind, something was bothering me but I couldn't lay a finger on what it was. After milking, at about half past five, it was almost as if someone was saying to me, 'Go and check the donkeys.' The thought just rattled round in my head, 'Go and check the donkeys, go and check the donkeys.' I jumped in my car and drove out to the field.

Pulling up I saw a group of noisy children milling around the animals; they took one look at me and ran off. From the road I could see that the animals were injured so slowly and carefully, talking gently all the time, I walked over to the horse and donkeys. All four of them had been tied up with string and wire, their coats were scuffed with shoe marks and mud, the sticks they'd been beaten with lay discarded on the ground. Beautiful, gentle Mimi was in a bad way, and Major, my wonderful, loyal horse, was standing on only three legs, its fourth suspended in mid air. I drove back home, phoned for Peter to come to help and have the vet on stand-by, raced back to the field with a horsebox and loaded them all up.

Major, my horse, had a broken bone in his leg and had to be put down. It was heartbreaking. I said to the vet, Mr Trump, 'What about Mimi?' He took a deep breath, and sighing said, 'Heather, I can't do anything. She's near foaling so we will just have to wait.'

That night I could hardly sleep. How could children be so cruel? How could they beat a living creature so hard without realising the pain it would cause? I had to find a way of making sure they understood how much suffering they had caused. By daybreak an idea had formed in my mind.

At 8.30 the following morning I marched into the village school, cornered the headmaster, and said, 'I'd like to go into assembly to talk to the children.' He listened to my sad and horrible story, and could see I was angry and upset, but he said he didn't think there was anything he could do about it. It soon became clear to me that he had no intention of allowing me to disrupt his timetable. 'I'm sorry,' he said, 'But we have a pretty hectic day ahead of us. We have a Governor's meeting this evening. We'll talk about it then.' He stood up, took my arm and started to lead me to the door. Trying to control my temper I took a deep breath, swung round and looked him straight in the eyes and said, 'If you don't let me talk to those children right now I'll call the police. I've had to have my beautiful horse put down and now I'm waiting to see what happens to my donkeys when they foal. I saw some of your children running away. You choose. Either I go into that hall or I'm off to the police station straight away.' That shut him up. He quickly backed down and led me into the school hall to address the assembled children.

'Some of you children know what you were up to yesterday teatime and I'm sure you'd like your friends to know what you were doing. I'd like to tell those of you who came into my field that the vet had to put down my horse last night. Do you know what that means? Yes, the vet had to kill him. Do you know why the vet had to kill him? It was because he had a broken bone in his leg, because some of you came into my field and cruelly beat my animals with sticks and wire. Whoever did this left my three donkeys badly injured and two of them should be having baby foals quite soon. I don't know what will happen to them, they might die' That's all I said. I was too upset to say any more. You could have heard a pin drop. I slowly looked at each individual child. There were some very red faces. I never had any problems with schoolchildren after that.

I nursed Mimi for two long and harrowing weeks, making her as comfortable as possible until she went into labour. She was so exhausted and ill afterwards that she just lay there struggling to breathe, her newly born jack foal beside her. The vet said, 'Heather, five or ten minutes at the most. That's all she's going to last.' Kneeling down in the muck I held her and hugged her, talked to her and kissed her, and cuddled her in my arms until she died.

Mr Trump looked at me sadly and said, 'I'll put the jack foal down, Heather.' I looked at that tiny bit of skin and bones, still slimy and bloody, steaming in the hay, took a deep breath and said, 'No, you don't. I'll try and hand feed him.' 'You'll never do that,' he said, 'He's far too weak.' I carefully lifted him, carried him into the house and placed him on a pile of old blankets. Next I went out to the shed to collect an old playpen, filled it with more blankets and sat the donkey in the middle of it in the corner of our huge sitting room. Then the old fire-guard came out of store and I kept the fire burning day and night. Every hour for the first few days I fed him with Ostermilk. For a full week I slept by his side and gradually he began to thrive. I named him Timothy.

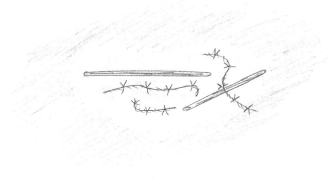

© Ken Parradine

Martha with her foal at a later date

Nature provides

We've never been big drinkers but I loved making home made wine - potato wine, wheat wine, carrot wine, elder flower, dandelion, elderberry, parsley, rhubarb, apple, plum, pear, blackberry and sloe wine. By scouring the hedgerows for fruit I would make up to 50 gallons a year, most of which I gave away to family and friends. It was a lovely thing to do, turning ripe and luscious fruit into delicious wine, and I found it very therapeutic. Nature provides so much for us and you can so easily make use of it.

'Are you in tonight, or out?' asked young Peter, as I washed up the dishes in the kitchen. 'Your Dad and I are going out together tonight and I'm really looking forward to it.' It was very rare for us to have time to spend together away from the home because there was always either one or both of us working with the animals. 'Anyway, why do you want to know if we're in or out?' I queried, 'Do you want a lift somewhere?' 'No,' said young Peter, 'It's just that I've asked the gang around to play football. Is that all right?' 'Of course it is, you know your friends are always welcome.' And off I went to get myself ready.

As we set off in the van I could see the clouds gathering in the West and knew it wouldn't be long before the rain arrived. 'Oh, well,' I thought. 'It looks as though the football will be off.' 'I think Stowell could be in for a noisy night,' said Peter as the first drop of rain landed on the car windscreen, 'It wont be too long before play is suspended and they'll be inside the house with the record player blaring out. I'm glad we've escaped.'

Returning home as we rounded the corner we could see what looked like every light in the house blazing out into the dark, wet night. The windows in the sitting room were thrown wide open, the curtains billowing about inside but from the car we couldn't see a single person. 'Very odd,' I thought.

We walked up the path and the mystery deepened - there against the wall was a line of bicycles. 'They can't have gone home, Peter,' I said, anxiously looking around. It was oddly quiet, all we could hear was the thump, thump, thump of the pop music. Tiptoe-ing quietly we pushed open the sitting room door and there on the floor lay ten sleeping boys, out for the count, surrounded by what looked like dozens of empty wine bottles scattered everywhere.

I had a lot of explaining to do to anxious parents later that night!

© Ken Parradine

Wedding Day. 28th Novermber, 1959.

One week before Susan was born.

64

Heather and Peter.

Heather, Susan, Peter and Young Peter.

The family in 1975

Timmy and Christopher

Timmy the donkey became part of the family and soon started to behave like one of the dogs. The donkey and the three dogs scampered round happily together and even when it came to resting Timmy would snuggle down alongside them to make one big happy heap of contentment.

'Lost in Space' was on the television at that time and the children absolutely adored the programme. When it was time for it to start Susan, Peter and Robert would come running into the sitting room, switch on the television, and leap onto the sofa. As soon as Timmy heard the programme music his ears would prick up, his head would go on one side as he listened intently, then with a rush he would run towards the sofa, take one big jump, and land beside the children. Then the pushing and shoving and wriggling would start and he wouldn't settle down until he was sitting bang in the middle with an uninterrupted view of the television screen.

Just before Christmas I went into Yeovil, did my shopping and left Peter to go to the livestock market in the town. When we met up he was smiling from ear to ear, 'Guess what I've bought the children for Christmas?' he said. 'What now?' I thought, dreading the worst. 'You're sure it's something they'll like?' I asked him. 'I've bought a Shetland pony 34" high. He is beautiful. They'll love him.'

He was a wonderful rich chestnut brown with a beautiful cream mane and tail, such a contrast; even his hooves were a lovely pale cream. We named him Christopher, he was introduced to Timmy and they got on like a house on fire. So the pony moved into the house along with the donkey, the dogs, the children and both my parents. Each night as soon as I said, 'bed' all the animals walked over to their blankets, lay down and didn't move until I disturbed them in the morning. 'Come on, out for your poos,' I shouted and out they would all go. They never had an accident inside.

Peter our eldest boy was a sensitive child but Robert was a tough little lad and he took one look at the Shetland pony, jumped on its back and had a quick ride round the kitchen table. Peter was thrilled to have such a beautiful, gentle creature to play with, and summoning up all his courage climbed carefully on to Christopher's back. 'Gee up,' he said, and immediately fell off onto the kitchen floor with a loud thump. Rubbing his bruised bottom he stood up, brushed away the tears and said, 'I'm not sure I want Christopher as a Christmas present,' he said, 'Can my half go back ?' 'You'll soon learn how to ride him, dry your eyes, and you can have the first turn at feeding him,' I said. In a short time they both loved the pony and took it in turns to groom him.

I loved making cakes for the family. One morning I iced a beautiful big chocolate cake, decorated it, and set it bang in the middle of the kitchen table. It was a huge table, seating ten people comfortably, and having animals in the house made me decide to build a barricade round it, to protect it from their hungry mouths. I carefully arranged all the ten chairs around the perimeter of the table, adding some more to fill in the gaps, and I was quite satisfied that nothing could get at the cake. Off I went to milk the cows. When I returned all but one of the chairs had been pushed out of the way and in the middle of the table was a tiny piece of round cake - the only bit Timmy and Christopher couldn't reach!

One day Timmy stood on a nail so I rang the Vet's in Sherborne and was asked to take him in to the surgery. I opened the back of the estate car but this time he was too uncomfortable to climb in by himself, as he usually did, so I had to push him in the best I could. We arrived at the Vet's and it was full of people patiently waiting with their dogs, cats and rabbits. As I walked in with my donkey on a lead there was a stunned silence. You should have seen their faces.

Unfortunately Timmy got very, very protective, despite being castrated, and he and the Shetland pony started to get very boisterous in the house so the time came for them to be put out in the field with some Jennies. When the children had birthday parties their friends loved to ride the donkeys but I always said that they must not ride Timmy. Sue our daughter was about 13 then, and a bit of a show-off, and decided to ignore me. Confidently she mounted him; he wasn't having any of it and bolted down the field, slipped on a cow's pancake and deposited Sue bang in the middle of the stinking heap. She vowed never again to ride on a donkey - and I don't think she did.

Gradually the donkeys grew older and Timmy grew wilder and more confident. Robert was instructed never, ever to take his friends anywhere near him and on no account should they attempt to sit on any of the other donkeys. I was busy in the house when suddenly I heard, 'Help. Help. Help. Mrs Moorse, come quick.' With our hearts in our mouths Peter and I ran up the field to see Robert flat on his back with Timmy kneeling on his chest. It was a horrible sight; blood was trickling down his leg and Robert lay moaning on the damp grass surrounded by his shocked friends. I grasping Timmy firmly and pulled him off, Peter picked up our terrified son, bundled him into the car with his leg swathed in bandages and drove at top speed to the local hospital. The Doctors were quite amused to see such injuries caused by a young donkey and Robert still bears the scar to this day - and he's now 40.

Eventually Timmy became so protective that the time came for him to go to another home. I think he thought I was his mother and he wouldn't let anyone near me. One day I heard of a gentleman who lived at Bagber near Sturminster Newton and he was looking for a donkey as a companion for his filly. Timmy went to live at his new home and settled down very well with his friend the horse.

Many years later when I was awarded the Queen Victoria Medal by the RSPCA for my 'long and meritorious service in the cause of animal welfare,' the lady reporter who came to interview me for the Blackmore Vale Magazine was fascinated by my stories. When it came to the story of Timmy and the cake she looked at me with a huge smile on her face and said, 'Do you know, the gentleman who took Timmy in was my father. And each market day he would buy three iced buns; one for Timmy, one for his horse and one for himself.'

Food

I never set out to open an animal rescue centre - it just sort of happened. By word of mouth my name and reputation for caring for sick, ill, unwanted and injured animals became well known. The telephone would ring day and night and almost every day I would come across a box of animals, or even boxes, left outside the gate and I never knew what was cooped up inside waiting for my attention.

After checking them over very carefully the first thing I did was to feed them. Many of the poor things deposited on my doorstep were suffering from malnutrition and were desperate for food. For many years I bought the animal feed stuff out of the family budget but financially it was a bit of a struggle.

Country people are very kind and generous, they recognised the work I did and, many of them being farmers meant that they understood just how much it was costing me to support and care for the animals. Often the doorknocker would sound and there, on the doorstep, would be cans of food, bales of hay and bags of nuts. And occasionally, when I popped into the local village shop, I would return to the car and find some kind soul had anonymously deposited on the car seat some food or other for the animals to eat.

One day, after taking some starving guinea pigs from a lady dripping in diamonds, I decided to have a bit of a think about how I was paying for animal food. *After discussing it with Peter I decided to ask for donations but my requests were not always well received. As long as some of them were getting rid of their animals they weren't concerned with the next stage. It was very much, 'out of sight, out of mind,' for many. The donations didn't really add up to much, they helped, but in no way met all the bills I had to pay.*

I never took in dogs or cats, or ferrets, but I provided telephone numbers of animal rescues who could take them in.

Rabbits

It was the fourth telephone call I'd had that day and the woman sounded hysterical. 'Please, please can you help me,' she said. 'I just don't know what to do. I've phoned the pet shop and they weren't very helpful and a friend said that you might be able to help.' 'You'd better tell me what the problem is,' I said. 'It's the rabbit. It stinks. I can't stand it any more. My husband says he'll bash it on the head if it's still here when he gets in from work. Will you have it.' Another one, I thought, 'Yes, you'd better bring it over right away.'

The blue Volvo estate car pulled up outside the house and a large, important looking lady came striding up the path. Banging imperiously on the door she stood there, hands on hips, waiting for me to dance attention on her. 'You'll have to come and get it,' she said. 'I've a bad back, I'm not supposed to lift anything.'

The boot lid was opened to reveal a large baked bean cardboard box. I lifted it out, put it on the floor, and was just about to look inside when she slammed the boot shut, rushed round to the driver's seat, climbed inside and shouted through the window, 'I'm not standing here while you open that box. The smell is unbelievable.' And with that she drove away.

On opening the box I knew immediately what the problem was, the rabbit had something called fly strike. I picked her up, turned her over, and maggots were eating all her stomach. People put rabbits in hutches and often don't clean them out, big meat flies are attracted to the mess, lay eggs in the rabbits' fur and if it's a hot day within twenty four hours the eggs hatch into maggots and they eat their way into the rabbit's flesh. There was nothing I could do, I just took it to the vet's and he put it down. I had to pay for it; the woman hadn't left a penny!

Poor rabbits seem to suffer from neglect more than most animals. Teeth are a problem to them and I have had them brought to me with twisted teeth growing right through the nose and on one occasion I had one poor creature with teeth growing out of each of its eyes. If you're buying a rabbit the first thing you should look at is its teeth. If the top set are growing out over the bottom you will have trouble, they will continually grow because they are not grinding together. But most of this problem is caused by in-breeding and if people think they are going to make money by breeding animals they don't care whether they are good specimens or bad specimens.

I had a fantastic vet for a number of years and he would give me 25% off the bill and if I had a rabbit that had been badly neglected, or somebody had dumped it, I would ring him up. All I had to say was, 'I need your help,' and he would fit me in however busy the practice was and 60% of the time he never used to charge me. He was a real friend and a fantastic vet.

I often reached the stage when I thought I just couldn't take in any more animals but one look at the neglected filthy creatures soon melted my resolve. 'Just imagine what that poor thing's been through, through no fault of its own,' I'd say to myself. ' What's one more animal to care for?'

If there's one message that I can get across to people in this book it's this; before going out to buy any animal think long and hard about it. It's not for a week, it's not for a year, sometimes it's for a lifetime. Animals don't ask much of you but they do give back an incredible amount of love.

One Sunday afternoon I had an open house for people to come and enjoy looking at the rescued animals when Peter called me to say there was a young couple by the gate with a rabbit they wanted me to take. 'Not another rabbit,' I thought. 'Don't worry, I've told them you're full up and can't take any more.' Looking around to see if I could find a run for one more I turned to Peter and said, 'Tell them to come over here.'

Up walked this young lad and his girlfriend, carrying a rabbit, which they had seen kicked around like a football by a group of lads in a nearby village playing field. It was a large French lop rabbit with long dangly ears, its fur was matted with mud and blood, it was a right mess.

I always isolated the rabbits in case they were carrying any disease. So this lop was placed in a rabbit house and run, which was about 8 feet long, away from all the other rabbits. I left her to settle down with food and toys, with which to play, and didn't trouble her until the following morning when I took her a fresh bowl of food. As I put my hand inside the run her front paw shot out and her long unkempt nails ripped my hand to shreds. She was terrified of humans. It took six whole weeks to build up her trust and then I introduced her to a castrated male, and then a few days later to a group of three or four other rabbits, and she settled down beautifully.

But sometimes the phone would ring and it would be someone wanting a rabbit as a pet for their children. It was a very rare occasion when I allowed this to happen. The first thing I would ask was, 'Where will you keep it?' If they replied that it would be in a hutch I would say, 'Sorry, you're not having a rabbit from here.' I've belonged to the Somerset East RSPCA for years and at one meeting someone said, 'Huh! You have more of a job to get a rabbit or guinea pig from Heather than you have from the RSPCA. She gives you the third degree.'

Not all children, but some children, don't realise that rabbits have to be fed twice a day; they have to be cleaned out regularly, most of them have to be groomed and they need a house and run and things to play with, just like a child, so they will be happy and healthy.

Starter kits for rabbits and guinea pigs are an abomination. They are about 3 ½ feet wide, 2 feet deep and 2 feet high, and come complete with a bit of bedding and food and with a feeding bottle attached to the wire front. One day the strident voice of a woman came over the phone, 'My daughter's going away to college and we don't want the rabbit any more. Can I bring it over.' 'Yes,' I replied, 'But I'd appreciate a small donation because it will probably need to have a couple of injections, one for myxomatosis and one for a viral disease.' You can have a

Hanging baskets ready for Open Day.

Sparky

There's something about parrots that fascinate me. The African grey is my favourite and I had a friend who rescued them, made them well and then sold them on to make room for more. Some of them given to him were in appalling condition. I went along one day and saw this African grey in a small cage - he'd left it there so I could see how it was brought in to him. The cage was about 2 feet square and it was half full of silver milk bottle tops, put in there for the poor thing to play with. Its body was covered with bald patches and a few pathetic feathers sprouted here and there. I knew I had to take him home, bring him back to full health and give him the companionship of the other parrots I was caring for.

At the same time I had a blue and gold macaw parrot, named Henry, and Charlie whom I've still got, and another two African greys, all of which I kept in large cages in my kitchen diner. Every day, at a certain time, they were allowed to fly in and out of the cage as they wished. People reading this must think my house was filthy, but it wasn't. It's very easy to keep clean if you clear up as you go along. If you keep animals they have to feel happy and secure, to have freedom but also have the security of a 'home'.

One day, I had all my parrots out in the kitchen walking about on the top of the cages, and as they hopped about above me I was witnessing the mess I'd have to clear up when they went back inside. I was feeling particularly exasperated with them. I stood there with my hands on my hips and shouted at the top of my voice, 'Bloody parrots! Who'd have them? Just look at the mess. Back in your cages.' And I clapped my hands together to shoo them inside.

Suddenly there was a loud knock on the door. Annoyed at being disturbed I threw the door open so wide it cracked on its hinges and there stood an RSPCA officer in his full uniform accompanied by a student. They'd come to make sure I was looking after all the animals properly before the open day and there I'd been shouting my head off. I didn't know what to do. Would they say I wasn't a fit enough person to care for animals? He looked at me sternly and said, ' I heard what you said just then.' Then he gave a great big smile. 'Bloody parrots! I often say just the same thing!'

'You've a lovely collection of parrots, Heather, he said as he looked into the cages, 'I don't suppose you'd like another one, would you? I've just had an African grey handed in.' 'Does it need a lot of attention?' I enquired. 'The chap who owned it died last week and when the daughter went in the parrot was found on its dead owner's body; they were the best of friends. The family won't have anything to do with it.' 'The poor little thing! Of course I'll take it.' I said. 'It's obviously used to human love.'

The following day Sparky, as he was called, arrived in a magnificent cage and he soon settled down with the other parrots. Some days later mother and I were sitting quietly in the kitchen having a cup of tea when the phone rang. Before we could answer the voice of an elderly man rang out loud and clear, 'Answer the bloody phone you silly old cow.' Then this horrible smoker's like cough began emanating from the birdcage - it was Sparky.

Sparky's language was horrendous and it soon became obvious that he was repeating the way the old man had spoken to his wife. If anybody came to visit it would trigger him off and out would come this stream of foul language. I couldn't repeat the words he used - bloody, bugger and sod it paled into insignificance alongside his rich language. After about six months he seemed to forget the worst words and used only the ones he heard from me. He became a very happy and contented parrot, especially after I put him with a female grey, and they lived happily together for thirteen years until he died from a stroke.

Answer the bloody phone :— . . .

Sparky

Fire

For many years bonfire night was a very special night at Dyke's Farm. Peter and the children built an enormous bonfire in the paddock and we invited all our friends and their children to join in the festivities. I made soup, sausage rolls, pasties, jacket potatoes, bacon and egg pies, cakes, biscuits and treacle toffee which the children loved. It was always a special evening and one that we all looked forward to as the nights began to draw in. But it wasn't to be repeated for ever.

One day I was in the kitchen cooking chips when the doorknocker went. I pushed the chip pan to the back of the stove and went to answer the door. This time it wasn't someone delivering an animal for me to care for; it was a neighbour who'd called to buy some eggs. I went out to the store, packed up a dozen eggs, handed them over and set off back to the kitchen to continue cooking supper.

As I walked down the corridor I thought, 'That's a peculiar smell. I wonder if Peter is spraying the fields with something different?' I opened the kitchen door and saw, to my horror, that the chip pan was on fire. The flames had leapt to the ceiling, the polystyrene tiles were burning, and droplets of burning plastic were setting fire to the carpet starting up their own little fires. The smoke was so thick I could hardly breathe and I could hear young Peter screaming somewhere but I couldn't see him. 'Where are you Peter? Where are you?' I screamed. I was coughing and choking and the smoke was so dense I couldn't see my way across the room.

I was trapped, I couldn't breathe, where was young Peter ....then I collapsed.

I came round in the front room with a lovely young toy-boy fireman leaning over me administering oxygen. I thought I'd gone to heaven! There by the side of him stood all three children and Peter. I was so very thankful. But it was the children who'd saved the day because they'd been playing in the fields and had seen smoke billowing out of the kitchen window, and that had been when I heard young Peter screaming. They'd rushed through the front door, spotted my legs through the smoke of the kitchen and dialled 999.

A fire is a terrible thing. Smoke permeates everything. The whole house was black inside and had to be decorated throughout. Cobwebs I didn't know were there were enhanced by the thick black smoke and seemed to wave at me as they gently moved in the wind blowing through the open windows. I vowed I'd never cook chips again.

Unfortunately that was the end of our bonfire parties - I could never again face seeing anything burning so wildly. I shall never forget young Peter screaming, and what might have happened.

© *Ken Parradine*

Rosie

'My blasted cat has brought in a baby bird,' said the lady on the phone, 'I think it's a blackbird. Will you take it, Heather?' 'Yes, but bring four tins of dog meat with you.' 'Dog meat? Why, are your dogs hungry?' 'No, it's to feed the bird on.' 'Well, I've never heard of anything like that before,' she said, 'Are you sure?' 'You just bring it along and I'll show you.'

At about 2 o'clock she turned up with this little blackbird which looked as if it had just flown the nest. 'My four cats have been eyeing this poor little thing all morning,' she said. 'I'm very relieved to be handing it over but it has been mauled a bit.'

She was spot on there; it had been mauled 'a bit'. Its head was hanging limply on one side and its feathers were matted together with blobs of blood. I didn't hold out much hope for this one surviving.

After cleaning it up and feeding it with the dog meat I put it into what I called my hospital box - a wooden box somebody had made for me with little electric wires running through the base to keep birds warm. It was a stubborn little thing when it came to feeding time. It wouldn't open its mouth for the dog meat and trying to drop a mealworm down its throat was very frustrating. The first time I attempted to feed her it seemed to take hours and it was two days before she got the knack of it.

A rabbit suffering from fly strike.

Toys for the rabbits.

Fred & Jimmy.

Owls and kestrels

The RSPCA and I often worked very closely together. Members of the public would occasionally take in to them injured kestrels or owls, which would firstly be taken to the vet's to be checked over and then brought to me to care for them. In those early days to keep birds of prey you had to have a special license from the Post Office costing £8. Most kestrels had been stunned by flying into traffic and after a few weeks, when I knew they were well and able to care for themselves, I opened the aviary doors and released them back into the wild.

Vets would also approach me directly to say they'd had a bird left, they'd had to take a wing off and, as it couldn't fly from predators, would I take it in? Many people think that such injured birds should be put down because they cannot fly but I had some fantastic aviaries built with tree trunks reaching up to perches so that they could hop up and down. Great big boxes and barrels were on the floor for them to shelter inside, there were bushes and shrubs for them to explore, and they always had plenty to eat.

I love owls. I kept injured barn owls and tawny owls, and I bought myself a pair of three-month-old European eagle owls which were housed in a huge aviary built specially for them. I fed them each day on dead chicks which were kept in a special freezer. If I was driving along and came across a newly killed bird, or a rabbit, at the side of the road I stopped and popped it into the back of the car to feed the owls with later.

For three years I nurtured my beautiful Eagle owls and to my delight I noticed they had built a nest, the female was sitting on it, a sure signal to the male that she was ready to breed. Each morning I eagerly visited the aviary, dropped in some food, and peered closely at the nest looking for eggs.

One morning I was very puzzled to noticed a hole in the wire of one of the aviaries. 'A fox,' I thought. Angrily I marched up to the wire and peered inside. There on the floor were two dead little owls, but no fox had found a way in, a human had visited in the dead of night, cut through the wire, and rung their necks. It had been a carefully planned attack.

I was so shocked I could hardly speak and sat for a while to rest, until I could summon up the willpower to check the rest of the birds. In the European eagle aviary poisoned meat had been thrown on the ground; next door in the tawny owl aviary lay the same foul substance but fortunately none of the birds had eaten any. I felt sick, how could anyone do such a thing to innocent harmless birds?

I reported the matter to the local police who said that they thought it was someone with a grudge, someone jealous of my ability to care for birds of prey. If that were the case it is something I just cannot understand. How can jealousy of someone's ability to rear injured creatures turn into the murdering of the creature you are jealous of?

I didn't know what to do. I loved those birds of prey but I decided that I couldn't bear to risk such a thing happening again. Within three days I had found good, caring homes for all the remaining kestrels and owls but their empty aviaries were a great sadness to me for many weeks to come.

© Ken Parradine

Official

It's funny, isn't it, sometimes you meet someone for the first time and they really annoy you, you can't put a finger on what has caused you to feel like that, and then when you get to know them better you find that they are wonderful people.

I arrived at the RSPCA meeting on the care of birds and small animals very early because I wanted to talk to the officer. To my surprise there was another visitor there before me who was chatting away very knowledgeably. I tried to join in the conversation but each time she wasn't keen to listen to my point of view.

About twelve months later this same girl turned up at Sunnyridge with two chinchillas. 'Hello,' she said as she stood there with a cardboard box in her hand, 'Maggie from the RSPCA said you'd probably be able to look after these two chinchillas.' I stood there for a moment waiting for her to recognise me but she was far too interested in stroking and petting the chinchillas.

After a short while, puzzled that I hadn't said anything in reply, she looked me in the face. That gave me the opportunity I needed, 'I know you,' I said, 'I remember you. You were at the RSPCA meeting and you upset me that night. I'm telling you to your face, because I don't say anything behind people's backs, if you upset me today I'll tell you. Now you've come you might as well see everything here.' 'Oh, no,' she said, looking very unsure of herself. 'That's not necessary.' 'Oh, yes it is,' I insisted, 'You will see every animal and the way I keep them,' and I marched her round every animal pen, run and house.

At the top of the garden I had just erected a fowl house for the rabbits with a big run so they could come and go as they pleased, and it had cost me £130. I had about 15 rabbits in there at the time and I explained that I was saving money to buy another one. 'I'll buy it for you,' she said. By now she was so embarrassed by the enormity of her foolish comments she would do anything to please me. 'Nobody buys anything for me,' I replied. 'It's for the animals I care for, and I choose when and what I'll buy. I'm a very independent lady.'

From that day onwards we became the best of friends and she was incredibly supportive and kind. Once when Peter was rushed into hospital, as soon as she heard of our predicament, she offered to collect me and my daughter and drive us all the way to Yeovil. We had experienced some exceptionally heavy rainfall and some of the lanes around Stowell were flooded, as was often the case. She had to negotiate her way through the countryside until she found a way of reaching us. It was 1 o'clock in the morning.

Every Saturday she came to help me with the animals and never came without three 25 kilo bags of carrots. She became a wonderful supporter of the animal rescue and once drove me all the way to Cornwall to collect Tilley and Blue, my beautiful whippets.

One Sunday morning she rang me to ask if she could bring her mother, Jean, to look at all the animals and see how they were cared for. Jean had been ill and so couldn't walk far and spent most of the time resting in the sitting room. It was an open day and the garden was full of visitors so I couldn't entertain her at all. She seemed quite happy sitting there and after two hours I went in and sat down to talk to her. Looking up she smiled at me and said, 'Heather, I've been told what wonderful work you are doing here for all those animals, and how you pay for everything out of your own pocket. I'd like to give you £1,000 to open a bank account for Sunnyridge Animal Rescue.' And that's how we became 'official'!

Sunnyridge Animal Rescue

The numbers of birds and animals rescued between 1997 - 2000

Degus	20
Racing pigeons	42
Hamsters	22
Tortoises	5
Toads	40
Baby bats	8
Red eared turtle	1
Rabbits	1500
Guinea pigs	300
Chinchillas	60
Hedgehogs	57
Assorted wild and aviary birds	505
Bronze turkey	1
Python	1
Toulouse geese	8
Potbellied pig	1
Sebastapol geese	6
African grey parrots	6
McCaw parrot	1
Lesser suphur cockatoos	2
Umbrella cockatoo	1
Donkeys	5
Goats	19
Geckos	3
Tree frogs	3
Woodpeckers	6
Kingfisher	1

Peter Moorse's collection of rare breeds of poultry also lived at Sunnyridge.

Pheasants	30 different breeds =	70
Poultry	70 different breeds =	1000
Runner ducks/drakes		100

Not for sale

'Hello, is that Mrs Moorse?' asked the man on the telephone. 'Yes,' I replied wondering what it was he was hoping to be able to get rid of to me. He had one of those oily voices, one that seemed to be trying desperately hard to be nice to me. ' I'm coming down to the West Country next week and I wondered if I can pop in to see your birds. I'm a bird fancier too and a friend of mine said you had a wonderful collection.' 'Ring me when you get down here, will you, and then I'll know what I'm doing,' I said, and with that I put down the receiver.

At the agreed time a few days later two men turned up and as I walked them round the garden the one with the oily voice appeared to be fascinated with the aviaries, asking me all kinds of questions, showing a real interest. He wanted to know everything. 'I'll be here all day at this rate,' I thought as we moved from pen to pen.

His friend, who didn't seem to be quite so enthusiastic, was a real nuisance and kept wandering off all the time. It was like having a naughty child in the garden. I like to keep my eyes on visitors to make sure they, in their ignorance, don't annoy the birds and animals. Time and again I shouted, 'Would you mind staying with us, please?' Reluctantly he re-joined us and shuffled along with his hands in his pockets. 'Oh, I'd like one of those parakeets,' he said. 'They are exquisite. How you much do you want for them. Just name your price?' I've had those two beauties for eighteen years, since they were babies, and I couldn't bear to part with them. I'm sorry but they're not for sale.' He seemed a bit disappointed. The two of them continued to walk round the aviaries and eventually left and went on their way.

Peter had once more been very ill in hospital and now he was back home. You never sleep well in hospital but that first night in his own bed he, and I, slept the sleep of the dead. The following morning I drew back the curtains, looked out into the garden automatically checking that all was well, and noticed a great big hole in one of the aviaries. I threw on some clothes and rushed up the garden to see what had happened.

Whilst we had been sleeping the sleep of the exhausted, thieves had visited. Where once had been a pair of Princess of Wales parakeets, and a pair of Rock Pepper parakeets, now stood empty aviaries; my double crested German trumpeter pigeons had also disappeared. All the birds that had been taken were very rare and valuable. In fact so rare were these birds that there was only one other man in the country who had any of these German trumpeter birds, and they were very desirable to opportunist thieves….and I had shown them round our collection so willingly. I knew who had stolen them but I couldn't prove anything.

Later that day a policeman cycled up on his bicycle and looked around for evidence as to how they had got into the back garden. You could see that the intruders had walked across the farmyard, round the silage clamps and right through the field - all the nettles and long grasses were trodden down. The policeman said he was sorry, he couldn't do much to help me. 'Well, there is one consolation,' I said. 'My two owl pigeons are still there in their aviary. Thank goodness they're almost black and the thieves wouldn't have been able to see them in the dark.' The policeman was a kindly soul but he did issue a warning, 'Heather,' he said, 'You have to be very careful. When people want to steal something they'll do it and won't care about attacking anyone who gets in their way. If you ever come across anyone trying to steal something, just be very, very careful and whatever you do don't confront them, just dial 999. We'll be round as quickly as we can. I don't really think I can give you any better advice than that.'

Two years later Peter and I went to a bird sale in Sherborne. As I walked round the hall admiring all the birds I heard a voice behind me which I thought I recognised. Turning round I saw this man in a dark mac. 'I know you from somewhere,' I thought but I couldn't quite place him. I stood there looking across at him, and over to me he came with a great big grin plastered across his face. 'Can you remember me?' he asked, as bold as brass. Then the penny dropped, it was him, the opportunist thief with the oily voice. 'I had your parakeets and pigeons,' he boasted, 'I stole them to order.'

© Ken Parradine

Voracious appetites

My kitchen windows had wonderful views over the garden and during the winter it was a joy to sit at the table watching the many wild birds living in the surrounding trees and hedges. I once logged twenty-eight different varieties and often friends called round to quietly observe their antics.

However plentiful Mother Nature is, during the winter all these birds needed feeding. Every fortnight they would eat 100 fat balls and to buy them would have been an added expense to my already stretched budget. 'Well,' I thought, 'I'll make my own. The children can help. It'll be a nice messy job for them.'

I saved the fat from cooked joints of meat and mixed it with lard, bits of grated cheese, and any old biscuits I could lay my hands on. With their sleeves rolled up the children delighted in putting their hands deep into the mixing bowl squishing and squashing the balls into shape. It was a wonderful way of keeping the three of them occupied on cold winter afternoons.

The birds loved suet, the hard fat from around animals' kidneys which butchers used to be able to sell but are now no longer able to. I also loved suet because I didn't have to do anything to it, I just hung it on the trees for the birds to enjoy. Instant food!

Sitting by the kitchen window counting the different species of birds with the children was great fun. Out on the side lawn I had fifteen wire bird feeders containing peanuts and seeds, not mixed up but separate, and the birds knew which feeders had what food in which. They ate their way through 25 kilos of peanuts a month plus all the other nuts and seeds. When you look at how small some of the wild birds are you marvel at where all that bird food went.

© *Ken Parradine*

Uninvited visitors strike again

Peter's main hobby was to keep rare breeds of poultry and at one time he had 70 different species and was often the only person in the country to have some of them. His favourite breed was the silver Kraienkoppe for which he paid £80 for a pair over 20 years ago, and he was very fond of his Cochins, Brahmas and Leghorns. Bird fanciers from all over the country would travel to view his collection. At one time he kept three game birds, the kind illegally used for cock fighting, and he had two females and one male. The male was a wonderful specimen and Peter was very proud of him.

One early winter evening, when it was almost dark, there was a loud knock on the door. 'Wouldn't it be nice to have a bit of peace and quiet?' I said to Peter as I dried my hands. He went to answer the door and I continued cooking but from where I was standing I could clearly see who our visitors were. Two men stood there and they were both real roughnecks, horrible looking shifty eyed individuals.

'Evening Governor,' said the smaller of the two, throwing his cigarette end onto the step, grinding it out with his foot, 'We've heard you have some game birds for sale.' 'Oh, have you?' said Peter trying to look casually at me with a worried look on his face. I didn't like the sight of them at all and gave Peter a warning look. 'What were you thinking of exactly?' I asked as I joined the group at the door, sensing exactly what these two scruffy looking individuals were after. 'I've heard you have a very fine cock bird. Just you name your price.'

Peter was horrified at the forwardness of their approach. How dare they come to him expecting to buy one of his precious and much loved birds so they could just throw it into one of their illegal cock fights. 'I don't sell cock birds,' he said, as politely as he possibly could. He was in danger of losing his temper and I didn't fancy his chances against either of these two characters. 'I only sell if they go as a pair, you see, the male and the female. Sorry, I can't help you.' And with that we closed the door, lit the fire, and settled down for a peaceful evening.

But the following morning the cock bird had gone!

Running an animal rescue can attract some pretty unpleasant people, something I can never understand. I decided one day to build a pond but I wanted one of those good big deep ones, not one of those pathetic little ones you see in garden shops. I dug an enormous hole and sunk into it the back of a fibreglass milk tanker - it was about 6 feet deep and 8 feet across. I kept goldfish in it, that was until one morning when I saw a thick crust of black oil with dozens and dozens of dead goldfish floating on the surface. An uninvited guest had once again paid us a visit during the night.

© Ken Parradine

Peter's rare breeds

Fund raising

It wasn't until 1997 that the Sunnyridge Animal Rescue had its own bank account and from that time onwards all the profits from the open days went towards food and veterinary care for the animals.

Each year the hamlet of Stowell became a very busy place as friends and neighbours gave their unstinting support. The Kingman family farmers owned the field opposite Sunnyridge and each year they allowed the very many visitors to park their cars there. Their farm trailers were driven to the village church and chairs, trestle tables and benches were loaded into them and delivered to our garden; they were a tremendous help.

Stowell is a very tricky place to find if you don't know the area. Although it is sign posted from all the main roads the journey there, to visitors, seems to go on forever. There are many dangerously sharp bends, confusing T junctions and high hedges. To the stranger, it can be a very difficult place to navigate to because the usual landmark, the church tower, cannot easily be seen. Added to that there are no street names, no pubs, no village school so it was very important to have big clear signs saying, 'Animal Rescue Open Day,' clearly placed pointing in the right direction.

I had two very generous ladies who donated piles and piles of assorted sandwiches, crisps, tea and coffee. Because I enjoyed baking I made 100 muffins and had friends who donated cakes for sale and cakes to eat. The refreshments were wonderful.

In the early days I only had about 30 visitors but on the last open day 2 years ago we had over 400 visitors between11 in the morning and five in the evening. Some people stayed the whole day because there was so much to see and do, and on leaving would ask the date of the next year's open day so that they could put the date in their diaries.

One year people generously gave a total of £2,500 which enabled me to care for many more birds and animals. I charged £1 entrance fee originally, then it went up to £2 and we had stalls for books, bric-a-brac, plants, cakes - all kinds of things and tea was served on the side lawn all day. The last time we opened we had a long queue of people waiting patiently to enter the garden and some had come from as far afield as Cornwall.

People were very kind and generous and I received ten bequests of money from the families of those who had died. I was always incredibly touched that at such a dreadful time of mourning they had thought about the work I was doing with the birds and animals.

© *Ken Parradine*

Armed for battle

The cowardly night-time prowlers made my life hell for nine long and terrifying months. Not only were my goldfish suffocated by oil, my owls and kestrels stolen or poisoned, I also had to spend many hours rounding up dozens of rabbits released from their runs. One morning I went out to feed the birds and, lifting the lid of the seed barrel, I could hardly believe my eyes; a whole tin of bright blue paint had been poured all over the bird seed rendering it inedible. It was a deliberate attempt to destroy my confidence. Why was I being targeted like this? Did someone hate me so much they had to take revenge on my birds and animals?

Later that night, when it became dark, I prowled around the garden determined to catch the culprits. As each branch creaked my heart was in my mouth and the warning from the policeman, not to take any action, loomed large in my head. There I was alone and unarmed patrolling in the dark garden not sure what kind of thugs were out there. I wanted to catch the people who were causing me so much misery; I couldn't live with such constant stress and cruelty. I had to find out who it was.

Two nights later as the full moon shone down on the garden I sat up in bed wide awake. Something had woken me, I sat there listening, jumping at each nighttime sound. So as not to disturb Peter I slipped out of the bedroom as quietly as I could, found an old coat to slip on top of my night-dress, and shoved my feet into a pair of wellies.

Out into the night I trod, slowly advancing on the animal pens, checking that all was well. All of a sudden the hairs on the back of my neck were prickling. I was terrified and swung round ready to confront the intruder. There was no-one there. But I could feel eyes watching me wherever I walked. Next to the owl aviaries my son had built a large wooden fort for the grandchildren to play in and by the side of it lay a large pick. Now, the police had said that whatever I did I must not attack anyone, otherwise I could be charged with assault. 'To hell with that,' I thought. 'If there's anyone out to get me I'll get him first.' And I brandished my weapon hoping that I'd frighten them off. I marched up and down swinging my pick menacingly, trying to look as big, strong and tough as I could but I was terrified, somebody's eyes were watching every move I made.

The trees and bushes were waving in the wind and the moonlight cast wild shadows on the garden. I have never been as frightened in all my life; my nerves were stretched to breaking point - those eyes were watching my every move. With a desperate last glance around I stumbled towards the house, dropped the pick by the back door, and ran inside to the arms of Peter. I was as white as a ghost and shaking from head to foot. 'Pour me a large whisky, Peter,' I gasped and swallowed it down in one long burning, reviving mouthful.

I hardly dare go out the following morning. What would I find? Would there be corpses of animals strewn around the garden? Would more foodstuffs have been ruined? With my heart beating nineteen to the dozen, I took a deep breath and stepped outside and walked cautiously down the garden path.

All was normal, nothing had happened, the birds were singing for their breakfasts, many hungry animals needed feeding, the sun was shining and nothing had been touched. 'Am I losing my marbles? Had I just been woken by a bad dream and the moonlight and ghostly trees had loomed larger than life to terrify me?' No, I knew that it hadn't been my imagination that had left me almost witless. Someone had been hiding near the owl aviaries, watching every move I made.

I methodically walked around the garden checking every aviary and run but didn't find anything out of place. Then my eyes were drawn to the grandchildren's fort, somewhere I hadn't previously looked. Peering in I nearly passed out. There in the gravel you could clearly see the imprints of where someone had been kneeling, watching me walking round swinging my pick. He must have been as terrified as I because I never had any trouble again.

© *Ken Parradine*

Adoption

It's amazing how many people seeing nice fluffy rabbits gambolling around their runs immediately feel the need to have their very own pet. All they think about is holding it, stroking it, playing with it and not the daily grind of caring. Many people are very competent at caring for animals and work as hard as I at assuring the very best for their pets. Unfortunately others aren't and think that a rabbit hutch, a few carrots and rabbit pellets is all that is needed.

But how could I possible tell the capabilities of the many people who asked for an animal? Did they have a large enough garden to house a hutch and run? Could they afford the cost of food and possibly veterinary fees? Would they be kind to the animals; would they feed them and groom them when necessary? I had to find a way of dealing with this difficult issue.

I was pondering this point one morning as I browsed through the newspaper. There, in front of me, was an advert for three children who needed adopting. 'Poor little things,' I thought as I read about their plight. Then I thought about all the checks that would have to take place before an adoption. The applicants would have to be interviewed, their homes would have to be inspected............'I could do that,' I thought excitedly, 'I could interview those who wanted to offer homes to the animals very carefully, go and see how they lived as a family, how they cared for any pets they might have, look at the size of their gardens.' An idea was forming in my mind.

From that time onwards everyone had to sign a Sunnyridge Animal Rescue adoption form which stated the care that should be given to each animal, the housing they had to provide and that the animal should be checked over by a vet. On the adoption form it also stated that once signed it gave me the right to do spot checks, that means to turn up unannounced, to make sure the animals were being properly cared for. Only twice, in the ten years I ran Sunnyridge, did I have to bring rabbits home and that was because they were kept in too small a hutch. They had a run but whenever I went they were shut in the hut and not allowed the freedom of the run, so, back to my garden they came.

So, anyone applying for one of my animals had firstly to go through quite a demanding process. I never 'sold' the animals. If anyone wanted to make a donation to the rescue I would gladly accept and occasionally people were very generous and would give me £50 but mostly it was only a pound or two. But that money didn't give them the right to care for the animals in any way they chose - I made very certain of that!

© Ken Parradine

Tempting bunnies

The garden sheds were beginning to look a bit neglected, the wet weather had taken its toll and they needed another coat of preservative. 'They don't look very smart,' I said to Peter one day as we walked together round the garden. 'I'll go into Yeovil this morning to one of the do-it-yourself shops and pick up a can of wood stain.' 'Don't forget that we have visitors coming this afternoon,' reminded Peter. 'Right, I'll go straight away, just as I am.' I said. I was dressed for work, and didn't have time to get changed into something smart; in fact I was looking a bit of a mess but I wanted to get there nice and early so I could get the job out of the way.

It was lovely and quiet when I arrived at the shop and I soon found exactly what I wanted. The store was one of those that has an animal section, selling things like rabbits, guinea pigs and hamsters and I always made a point of just checking to make sure they were being kept properly. The animals were kept in holding pens, quite legally, but I felt very sorry for the way they were all crammed in together.

As I walked over I noticed a family looking at a rather larger pen with rabbits happily running round and with a pretty little house for them to live in in the corner - I have to say the furry bright eyed creatures did look lovely. 'I want a rabbit,' said the youngest, who looked about eight years old. 'Just look at them Mum. They're so cuddly. Can I have one?' 'Yes, Mum,' said his older brother,' Can we have one? Philip at school has one and he says they're lovely to stroke.

The parents looked at each other, the boys kept on pestering them and in the end the mother said, ' Yes, you can have one. But I don't know what we'll keep it in.' 'Don't worry about that, sir,' said the shop assistant who'd been unpacking boxes nearby, 'We supply starter kits containing everything you need.' 'Great,' shouted the boys, jumping up and down with excitement. 'I want the one with the black and white patches on it,' said the younger of the two children. 'Can I have that one, Mum?' Dad said nothing.

The party moved over to choose the starter kits and I followed on behind. 'These are really good value for money,' said the shop assistant. 'You get the hutch and the water bottle, some bedding and a bit of food for the first few days. Everything you will need.' 'We'll have it,' said Mum. The boys cheered, father felt in his pocket for his wallet and a starter kit was duly reached for.

I couldn't hold my tongue any longer. 'Excuse me,' I interrupted, 'What the assistant hasn't told you is that small rabbit is going to outgrow that hutch within six to eight weeks. Then what are you going to do?' The shop assistant was furious, 'What do you know about keeping rabbits?' 'Not a lot,' I replied. 'You sell. I pick up the pieces. At the moment I care for 136 rabbits and most of them come from families who bought them on the spur of the moment and haven't a clue how to look after them.'

The children by this time were looking a bit puzzled by this strange, scruffy looking woman who was being a bit of a nuisance. 'What's she going on about, Mum? Can't we have one?' 'Some children are marvellous with pets,' I said looking down at them as kindly as I could, 'And you probably will be too. But they do take a lot of looking after. They have to be fed twice a day, every single day of the year, when it's raining and snowing and freezing cold and when you go on your holidays. Then you have to keep them clean. Twice a day you have to scrape out all the smelly droppings, all their poo.' 'Yuck,' said the bigger boy giving his brother a quick shove, 'That's your job.' 'But that's not fair,' replied his brother. 'Yes, it is, you chose it.'

By this time the parents were getting a bit fed up. 'Look,' I said, ' Some people buy animals on the spur of the moment without really thinking it through. Why don't you go and buy the boys a toy each, something they can play with that doesn't need looking after? Boys soon get fed up with feeding and cleaning and within a fortnight you'll be the ones at the bottom of the garden in the cold and wet; then you'll all start arguing about whose job it is. It'd be much easier to buy them both a toy, one they can push in a cupboard when they get bored with it.'

'Thank you,' said the father almost cheering with delight. 'That's the first bit of common sense I've heard all morning. You're right. They will get fed up with it very quickly. Come on lads, fancy a new football?' 'Can I have one of those new orange and black ones,' said one of them, 'Can I, Dad?' And off they happily went.

The assistant looked at me with daggers in her eyes - I should have been six feet under, and marched at a brisk pace across the shop floor. Gathering together the bits and pieces I'd bought I looked up and saw the shop assistant advancing towards me with two men, one the manager and the other the deputy manager, so their badges read. 'Don't you ever come here again, lady,' said the manager in a menacing voice, 'My colleague and I will escort you to the door.' 'At least I've saved one animal from being cruelly confined in a small hutch,' I said. And with my head held high I was marched off the premises.

© Ken Parradine

Many hands

'Come on, girls, time for a break,' I shouted as I carried a tray full of orange juice and home made biscuits out into the garden. Inside rabbit runs, aviaries, huts and outhouses was a group of dedicated helpers, girls who came every Saturday morning to help with the numerous tasks that needed attention. Each girl was responsible for a different shed, and I had twenty-two sheds in all, and they would clean out all the muck, put in new bedding, and top up the water and feed stuffs. They were completely trustworthy and I could just leave them to get on with the work. They travelled from Crewkerne, Templecombe, Sherborne, Gillingham and Wincanton - miles around - and cheerfully worked unpaid whatever the weather.

For many years I had struggled on my own but now I had a wonderful team in place. Three of the girls came from the same family and they were brilliant; they never let me down and always worked with cheerful dedication. Out of this group of youngsters three more went on to be vets and I like to think that what they learned at my hand helped them a little bit with their studies. But I was very proud of each and every one of them.

'It's my turn with the barrow. You've had it for ages,' complained one of them who'd carefully swept together an enormous pile of rabbit dung. This was a usual cry because the numbers of helpers had gradually swollen to

ten and they could never agree on who should have the next turn with the wheelbarrows.

'Peter,' I said. 'We've got to do something about this. They're lovely girls and I don't like to see them arguing like this.' 'Girls,' I promised at the end of one morning's work, 'When you arrive next Saturday you will each have your very own wheelbarrow.'

'My word, Mr Moorse, you're going to be busy,' said the assistant at Mole Valley Farmers as he loaded the van. 'It's not often we sell so many wheelbarrows in one go.' 'Ah, we have a lot of helpers and we want to make their jobs as easy as we can,' explained Peter.

The following Saturday morning I carefully lined up ten wheelbarrows, ten brooms, and fifteen hand brushes and dustpans - you should have seen the girls' faces when they arrived!

© *Ken Parradine*

Karen Horsey - helper - Saturday

Ann Gay - helper - Saturday

The gift

'My wife has lost a rabbit and she's really upset about it.' Explained the man on the phone. 'Oh, dear, didn't you fasten the hutch properly,' I asked as sympathetically as I could. 'No, I mean the rabbit's dead. I've been up to the pet shop and they've given me your number. Do you have one I can have? Snowy lived with us for ten years and we really miss her. The garden seems very empty.' 'I'll be in this afternoon if you want to come and see me,' I said, 'But I have to warn you that I shall want to know how much you know about looking after rabbits.'

Up rolled Garth and Eve. Garth was sporting a Victor Meldrew T shirt with the words 'I don't believe it' emblazoned across his chest. In looks he wasn't at all like the TV character of Victor Meldrew, but in personality he was. He was very outspoken and took a great of pleasure in winding me up. I used to describe him as a miserable old devil, much to his wife's amusement and he'd retaliate by greeting me with, 'How are you today, you miserable old sod?'

He and Eve worked tirelessly for the rescue over a number of years and Garth often tested the patience of visitors with his rather off the wall sense of humour. At one open day he was manning the bookstall wearing this huge striped hat, the kind guaranteed to make anyone grin, when a grumpy looking woman approached him. He took one look at her and bellowed at the top of his voice, 'Can't you put a smile on your face? You're a bit of a miserable looking woman, aren't you?' He wasn't known for his tact but was great fun to have around.

We soon became the best of friends and every Friday afternoon he and Eve called to see us and took great delight in looking at all the animals. Garth showed a keen interest in animal welfare, he was a kindred spirit, and was always making suggestions and looking at ways in which he could help.

'Bring your car over to work next Monday, Heather, we have loads of paving slabs that'll do nicely in front of that new hut of yours,' said Garth as he 'inspected' the latest rabbit compound. 'I'm sure you can make use of them.' 'It is getting a bit muddy,' I admitted. 'Yes, half a dozen or so would make all the difference.'

The following Monday Peter stood by the side of me looking into the car boot. 'You'll not get many in there. If he wants to get rid of a great big pile we'll have to borrow something a bit stronger than that to carry them in. ' I jumped into the car and set off to join Garth at his place of work.

There in the builder's yard stood a great big pile of paving stones and my car looked almost ready to crumple with the weight it was carrying. 'We'll just get a couple more in, Heather, and that will be your limit,' said Garth as he dusted his hands together. We were just finishing loading up the boot when a car drew up and out jumped the owner of the firm. He took one look in the car and said, 'What on earth do you think you are doing?' I felt dreadful. Was Garth going to lose his job because of me? With a great big grin on his face Garth said to his boss, 'I said you'd be delighted to donate some of these paving slabs to this lady who runs an animal rescue!'

Garth's boss, a delightful man, became extremely generous over the years and at open days he provided us with all kinds of things to sell from his stock of goods. He gave us stone ornaments, stone animals and stone clocks; he never charged us a penny, enabling us to make a good bit of money from his generosity.

We were all working hard in preparation for the Sunday open day when on the Friday before, as usual, Garth and Eve came round. 'You go inside, Eve, I just want to have a good walk round with Heather,' said Garth. 'Right I'll have the kettle boiling for when you get in.' We walked around all the animal runs and he wanted me to explain where each animal had come from and what, if any, their problems were. 'It's a good job they've come to you. You will look after them, won't you Heather?' That struck me as a curious thing to say as I'd spent my whole life looking after animals but I had to reassure him, 'For God's sake, Garth, you know I'll look after them.'

Back in the kitchen we sat there discussing the arrangements for the open day. Garth enquired, 'Have you got a nice big basket of fruit for the raffle prize, Heather?' as he munched away contentedly at his fourth chocolate digestive biscuit. I'll bring one over for you on Sunday.' 'Thanks, Garth, that's the very last prize I was looking for,' and contentedly I sat back, crossing the last job off the list in my mind.

Sunday morning came and Peter came over to me to say that Garth had turned up carrying a magnificent basket of fruit. 'But Heather,' he said, 'He   looks terrible, really poorly. He's just propping himself up against the wall and his breathing is awful.' 'Peter shook his head, 'He's just said the strangest of things. He said that he's had a good life and has enjoyed it. It's not a bit like him to talk like that, he must be feeling bad.' 'I'll just finish sweeping this lot up and I'll pop over to see him. Put the kettle on and get out his favourite biscuits. That'll cheer him up. '

I never did see Garth again. By the time I'd sorted out what I was dealing with he'd gone home and the following Tuesday he died. At his funeral service a collection was taken and all the money came to the Sunnyridge Animal Rescue - a wonderful thing to do.

© Ken Parradine

Farewell

I was often approached by people worried about an animal which they suspected was being neglected. I told them all the same thing, 'Contact the RSPCA, there's no need to give your personal details, just give them information about the animal and they will follow it up.'

But when you care for animals there always comes a time when an animal becomes ill and sometimes has to be put down. If an animal is dying, and you know the end is near, it doesn't need the added stress of being loaded into a car, driven for miles to a strange place with different smells and different people.

It is far, far better to pay the extra cost of having the vet come out to you. It is horrendous having to watch a vet giving that last and final injection but if the animal is at home you can hold them, you can talk to them, you can love them right to the very end.

I know that for many people to see their pet being put down is far too stressful, but they are thinking of themselves and not the animal. I feel very strongly that to be there at the end of a pet's life is the last act of love you can show for an animal. Many times my heart has been broken but I know it is the right thing to do.

© *Ken Parradine*

Peter and Heather with the beloved whippets

Basil

As well as helping with the animals Peter was head groundsman at Leweston School for fourteen years. Leweston School is a girls' boarding school run by nuns just outside Sherborne. The nuns knew how much I loved animals and if ever they saw a bird or small animal in distress they gave it to Peter to bring home.

One year the tree surgeons had been working in the school grounds. Usually they were very good and if trees had birds' nests in them they left doing any work on them until later in the year when the birds had flown their nests. Unfortunately this particular time they pollarded a tree with a nest in it and instead of hiding the sawn off branches and nest, as they could so easily have done, they took the nest to the nuns to ask for their advice.

Peter walked into Sunnyridge kitchen bearing yet another cardboard box, 'I've a present for you, Heather,' he said with a grin. I opened the lid and jumped back in horror, 'Oh, it's a mouse, take it away.' 'No, its not. Look at it properly.' Peering closely I could see that it was a baby squirrel. I put the box onto a hot water bottle, rolled up one of Peter's old socks, dropped in some tissue paper and went to get the Ideal milk to feed it with. Once the tiny squirrel opened his eyes he felt secure and it wasn't many days before he was making a nest inside Peter's sock.

Basil, as we called him, thrived and soon became too big for the box and was housed in a large cage in the kitchen. He was a very inquisitive creature and loved to be let out of his cage exploring or snuggling down amongst the cats and dogs, often pinching a bit of their bedding to add to his nest. He loved peanuts and became a bit of a nuisance because he took to hiding them in my flowerpots; there'd be soil all over the place.

I adored Basil because he was such a good little companion. His favourite place to hide was in the pocket of my body warmer, which I kept on a kitchen chair. He'd scramble up the table legs, onto the table, jump on the chair and make for the comfort and warmth of my pocket. He'd even come shopping with me. All I had to say was, 'Basil, Mum's going out,' and up he'd scramble into my pocket. People would often say, 'You've got a mouse in your pocket,' and I'd say, 'No, that's Basil. He's a squirrel.' And his little head would pop in and out to see where we were going. As we walked along he'd run down my trouser leg, out onto the ground to explore, and that's when I'd try to walk away and leave him there so that he could go back to his wild state. But I never got very far; you'd see this streak coming straight for me, up my trouser leg he'd go and back into my pocket.

Cyril was a friend of Peter's and he often called round to look at Peter's collection of rare birds. Visitors were always welcome, given a cup of tea and, as I loved making cakes, there was always a nice big slice ready and waiting for him. He was a large plump man and made himself very comfortable in the easy chair, his wide trouser legs flapping round his ankles as he eased himself into position. 'What's that in your pocket? It's moving.' 'Oh, that's Basil, my pet squirrel.' 'Don't you let it near me,' he said as Basil popped his head out inquisitively. 'Don't worry, he's quite happy where he is.' We sat there drinking our tea, discussing the price of rare birds, when all of a sudden Cyril gave a tremendous shriek. Jumping to his feet he knocked his cup and saucer flying to the floor, shook his trouser leg as hard as he could, and gave a great howl. 'I've got a bloody squirrel after my nuts.'

TELL THAT SQUIRREL HE IS NOT BURYING THESE NUTS!